the **Puppies**

A guide to selection, care,

nutrition, upbringing, training,

health, sports and play

Content

Foreword

You have probably bought this book because you're
thinking of getting a puppy in the near future. That's
reason enough for congratulations. After all, a cuddly
little animal will change your life completely. On the
one hand, nicer, but on the other hand, busier, at least
for the first few months. During this time you're going
to be laying the foundations for an intense, and usually
pleasurable, friendship between yourself and your dog.
Now is the moment to form your puppy's character. In
its first year, it will learn more than in the whole of the
rest of its life, and the impressions it gets now, will
stay with it forever. So it's important for your puppy to
get to know as many situations as possible, so that it
won't be afraid of trains, crowded streets, shops, big
dogs, cats, humans and the many other things it will be
confronted with later.

This book has been written to put the new dog-owner
on the right track towards a good relationship between
man and dog. It covers practical matters such as feeding,
care, its own part of the home and the prevention
of parasites, but it also pays attention to the various
phases in a puppy's life, dogs and children, as well as
an extensive section on up-bringing.

Knowing about these subjects will help you give your
pet a better life. The basis is in this book. As humans,
we must never forget that we have bound the dog to us.
We have domesticated it to help us hunt, guard our
property or simply just to be our companion. Thus we
have also taken on the responsibility to take good care
of the dog. As far as it can, it will also take good care
of us.

About Pets

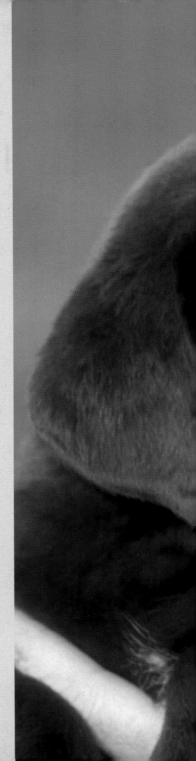

A Publication of About Pets.

Copyright © 2003
About Pets
co-publisher United Kingdom
Kingdom Books
PO9 5TL, England

ISBN 1852791950
First printing
September 2003

Original title: *de Praktische Puppywijzer*
© 2000 - 2002 Welzo Media Productions bv,
About Pets,
Warffum, the Netherlands
http://www.aboutpets.info

Photos:
M. de Blank,
R. Schellevis, J. Boes,
M. Kroon-Weber, Kingdom Books,
Isabelle Francios, N. Dronkers
and Rob Dekker

Printed in Italy

A puppy... what now?

The question comes up in almost every family at least once: "Should we get a dog? Dogs are affectionate, good and loyal companions, and puppies are fun to watch. Apart from that, they have a high 'cuddleability factor'.

Think before you buy

Never decide to buy a dog on impulse, even if it's love at first sight. Bringing a dog into your home means a lot of changes for the whole family. You're actually adding a new member of the family. Your new housemate must be walked, needs daily care and can't live on air. Moreover, it costs time and energy to turn a puppy into a well-trained, socialised dog.

There are plenty of reasons for a family not to buy a dog. On the other hand there are fewer reasons to actually do so... Firstly, never buy a dog as a toy for your children. Only ever buy one if you, yourself, want to because a child is absolutely not able to bring up a dog alone and to take responsibility for it. Once you've made up your mind to get a dog, then you must carefully consider what sort of dog best suits your family situation (breed, gender, size). Always keep the following points in mind:

• A puppy will often whine at night, certainly for the first few days;
• A puppy must be house-trained. It will certainly foul the house for several weeks (and this can go on until it's four or five months old);
• House-training and bringing up a puppy costs time and effort;
• A puppy must not be exerted to its maximum for the first year of its life;
• An adult dog must be walked at least three or four times a day, whatever the weather. At least one walk must be for thirty minutes to an hour;

- With a dog in the house, you can't simply go away for a weekend. Either you take it with you, or you have to find someone to look after it.
- A dog is a pack animal. It's not good for it to be alone a lot;
- Caring for a dog doesn't only cost time and energy; it also costs money. Reckon with costs between £ 300 and £ 600 a year (vet's bills, food and other expenses).

Golden rules for a good relationship

1. Your dog will always be your companion and most trusty friend.
2. A dog doesn't have human intelligence and can't think logically. But it will remember bad experiences.
3. If man and dog enjoy an enduring and intensive relationship, emotional ties will result.
4. Every dog is unique in terms of willingness to learn, adapt and relate to people.
5. Its owner must discover the dog's character, adapt to it and then help form and develop it.
6. A dog will learn to adapt to humans, and to perform certain tasks on command (sounds).
7. Never lose your self-control when dealing with your dog. Tact and love must always take priority.
8. A dog is a runner. It needs a lot of exercise to stay healthy. It will help train itself mentally by walking and exploring with the help of its nose.
9. Reward and punishment, at just the right moment, deliver the best results. But hitting a dog is altogether wrong, it will only ever produce the wrong results.

Taking your puppy home

You've found the pup of your dreams at a reliable breeder, and then you've set a date to pick your puppy up.

The puppy must be at least eight weeks old, because a good breeder will never separate his puppies from their mother before then. Don't forget to ask the breeder for a feeding plan, it's not a good idea to abruptly change a puppy's food.

The first days in its new home are an enormous change for your puppy. It needs all the attention and love it deserves. If you work during the week, arrange to pick up your puppy as early as possible on a Saturday morning. Then you-'ve got all weekend to give it your attention and to help your puppy get used to its new surroundings.

Ask the breeder not to feed your puppy that morning. You're proba-bly using a car to pick it up, and this is almost certainly its first car journey. With a full tummy, it will certainly be sick. Take someone with you when picking up your puppy, then, while you drive, the other person can sit holding it in his or her lap (on an old blanket). It's important for a puppy not to be sick during its first car journey. It will then regard riding in a car certainly as strange, but not as unpleasant, and it will get used to the car quicker. Adjust your dri-ving style to suit the circumstan-ces; avoid sudden braking, take corners carefully and don't accele-rate too hard. This will all help your puppy to view riding in the car as a pleasant experience. Towards the end of the journey, you may notice foam or slime around its nose and mouth. This is normal and is due to the tension of its first trip in the car.

May I introduce you...?

Once at home, carry your puppy inside in the right way. Never pick up a young dog by its forepaws, and never hold it with both hands around its little belly! Slide one hand under its chest and the other under its hindquarters. The puppy is then supported on all sides and can't wriggle its way out of your hands. Before you go indoors, see whether it want's to do its business at a spot you've picked. If it does, reward it immediately and effusively.

If your family includes (young) children, then they will all want to cuddle the puppy, pick it up, call it and play games with it. This is perfectly understandable, but don't permit it (however tough that may be). Your puppy must quietly come to itself. Place a bowl of water at its new, fixed place. Food is not necessary yet, that will come in the evening. Bring your puppy to its water bowl and let it take a drink in peace. If it doesn't want to, don't try to force it. You have to keep remembering that for your puppy everything is totally strange, and it first wants to check everything out and be sure it's safe. But a dog can easily adapt completely and be happy within a few days, as long as you stick to the rules. Introduce your puppy to its sleeping place. This must certainly be dry and draught-free. Choose a place in the house where it's not laying in people's way, but where it can see everybody. The latter is most important, because your puppy will want to be sure that its pack is all together, and that it's part of that pack. Leave all doors open, except for those that it should never go through in the future. Give it all the time and opportunity it needs to explore its surroundings in peace. This also means that you should not call your puppy! Remember that within a couple of hours it has landed in a totally new situation; away from its mother, brother and sisters, away from its own bed, and away from all those familiar scents and sounds.

After some time, your puppy will certainly be tired. If you remain still, at some moment it will fall asleep somewhere in the room. This will certainly not be the place you picked as its bed. It will certainly get used to that too, but if it now falls asleep in a place it feels secure, this is a (preliminary) sign that it's no longer quite so frightened. For the time being, stick to the feeding times the breeder has given you. An eight-week old puppy must certainly be fed four times a day. If you stick to the rule that it should go its own way as much as possible the first few days, your puppy will quickly get used to its new home. But you need to be nearby and teach it what it may and may not do in the house, and what is dan-

gerous for it. A clear 'No!' while quietly but firmly pushing it away from the scene of the crime is sufficient, as long as you repeat it often enough.

Perils of the night

The first nights in its new surroundings are an awful experience for your puppy. After all, it was used to being safe and sound together with its mother, and its brothers and sisters. Now they're all gone, and it's quiet and cold. So there will almost certainly be some whining and wailing. Be careful to make sure that you keep your puppy awake for the last hour before bedtime. A young dog that's been dozing under a chair from eight o'clock till eleven, and then has to go to bed, will find it very difficult to sleep.

Tip!
Wrap a ticking clock into an old towel and put this in the puppy's basket the first few nights. This will give the pup a sense of security by reminding it of its mother's heartbeat.

You may decide that your puppy should sleep at some place further away in the house, and it will certainly keep you awake with its constant whining. It is vital not to react to its noises, and these will normally stop after a few nights. If you do decide to let your puppy get used to sleeping alone, you

must accept a few disturbed nights. If you're fond of your sleep, put your puppy in an indoor kennel or an old box in your bedroom. Considering a dog's primeval instincts, this method is always more natural and responsible. A dog is a pack animal and at eight or nine weeks is unable to live alone, and is also not used to sleeping alone. In the wild, this level of self-dependence at such a young age would certainly lead to death. Due to the so-called 'imprinting' process, your puppy now regards you as a member of its pack (even if there's not yet a real bond). If you put it in a kennel in your bedroom, it can hear your breathing. Then all you need to do is murmur once in a while or stretch a hand out towards it to give it a sense of security. You can

put your puppy in its own sleeping place when it's a little older. By the eleventh week, it will be mentally ready for this. It's then more self-sufficient and knows its surroundings well, making it feel more secure. However, if your puppy only comes into the home at eleven or twelve weeks, don't take it to your bedroom with you. If you've already got another dog, let the puppy sleep with it, but make sure they don't play too wildly, because that's not good for your pup.

Letting your puppy sleep in an indoor kennel at the beginning has the positive side effect that it can't demolish anything while you sleep. It will also become house-trained at night faster, because dogs generally don't like fouling their own nest. A puppy will soon sleep through for five or six hours. At first this means you're out of bed early in the morning. The puppy's squeaks will wake you up. Talk to it so that the squeaks stop and carry it outside; it urgently needs its morning toilet.

Slowly and carefully, the nights can be extended. Anyone who claims that his or her puppy can go ten hours a night within a few weeks is doing something wrong. It's actually really bad for a puppy to have to hold its business for so long. It can even get itself into quite a state because it doesn't want to foul its own nest. Read more on this subject in the chapter "Upbringing".

Feeding your puppy

New-born puppies live on their mother's milk for the first three or four weeks, after which the breeder will slowly start to give them solid foods.

He will gradually increase this until the pups no longer take their mother's milk at an age of eight weeks. They are now 'weaned off'. As far as food is concerned, the puppy is no longer dependent on its mother when you take it home.

A healthy meal

Even after you have picked it up from the breeder, your puppy is still developing, both mentally and physically. A good, energy-rich food is extremely important. Puppy meal has a high nutritional value. A young dog grows very quickly and its body needs plenty of energy to help it grow healthily. Fast growth, though, does not mean you can let your dog get fat, so don't overfeed it. Feed an eight-week old puppy four times a day, but the amount of food that it

gets at each mealtime is rather small. Some people think that it's not enough and add a little more. This often leads to thin stools. When the puppy is given a little less to eat, its stools will quickly get back to normal.

Dogs of medium-sized and large breeds that get too fat are more vulnerable to problems with hip and elbow dysplasia (HD and ED), a sagging back or legs, and stomach disorders. To prevent this you must weigh your puppy once a week. Adjust the amount of food to its weight at that moment. Special puppy meal is available for puppies of large breeds. Apart from the scales, use your eyes to regulate feeding quantities. It's not necessarily a bad thing when people think their dog is too thin. If they talk of their 'nice chubby little dog', then there's definitely something wrong!

When you put its food bowl in front of it, your puppy should 'attack' it and wolf its food down. If it hasn't finished within ten minutes, it's had enough, so take the bowl away.

A healthy meal also means a healthy bowl, which is kept clean. Stainless steel bowls are ideal. Don't buy a bowl that is too small; not only will the portions grow, but your puppy's head too. Don't add any supplements to puppy meal. If you add calcium, for example, the calcium/energy balance in the food can be seriously distorted. This balance is important for proper development of a dog's bones. Mixing in fresh meat (heart and tripe) is also not advisable for the same reasons. Additions are more likely to cause harm than good so, for the first twelve months, use only ready-made manufactured foods.

How often to feed

From the moment you get your puppy home, it needs four meals per day. Once it's three months old, you can switch to three times per day. Once a dog is a year old, two meals per day are sufficient (mornings and evenings).
Use the guidelines printed on the food packaging as a guide to the quantity per meal/day.

The amount shown here is usually the result of breed, age and weight factors. But take care; these are only indications, and the amount your dog needs also depends on its energy consumption. This is not easy for the layman to judge however. You should be able to feel a dogs rib's if it has been fed properly; if you can't feel its ribs it is being overfed, and you must reduce the quantity, but you must also make sure it doesn't get too little food. Bigger breeds that are vulnerable to HD and ED must absolutely not be allowed to become overweight. There are often growth tables that have been established for these breeds, which your breeder can give you. There are also special foods for larger breeds, where the amount of calcium has been reduced in relation to the kilojoules.

Regular meal times will also help preserve your puppy's correct weight. Never give a dog extra food between meals because you think it may be hungry. It is also important that it eats its meal at once, otherwise it will become a fussy eater. Finally, it is extremely important that you never romp or run with your dog just after it's eaten. Leave it in peace for at least forty-five minutes to digest its food. Particularly bigger breeds run the risk of so-called stomach dilation (or stomach torsion or volvulus syndrome). This is a turning of the stomach, which closes

the stomach entrance and exit, trapping stomach gases. Only quick surgery can save your dog in the event of stomach torsion.

Changing your puppy's diet
Of course, you're free to switch over to a different food than your breeder gave you when you picked your puppy up, but do this in steps. Begin by mixing in a quarter of the new food with three-quarters of the old. After a week make it half / half, then another week later three-quarters new and one quarter old. The following week you can switch completely over to the new food. This method will make the changeover easier for your puppy to handle.
Of course, not every dog is the same. One thrives outstandingly well on a certain type of food, while another suffers from constant diarrhoea. If this happens to your puppy, stop using that food. Change its food until the diarrhoea stops (water, chicken and white bread or boiled rice gruel). Then revert to the food that the puppy was used to, or try something else. Don't let diarrhoea go on for longer than one day; a puppy can quickly become dehydrated! Consult your vet if diarrhoea continues.

It's virtually impossible for a layman to put together a complete, properly balanced diet for a puppy, so stick to manufactured foods. Certainly during the first

few months, feeding must be as consistent as possible. After six months, you can start to vary your puppy's diet with meal, mixer and canned foods of various makes. Your dog will now learn to eat other foods, and it won't be a drama if its own familiar food is not available on the odd occasion. The main element in its food must consist of dry chunks as these help to prevent dental problems. When on holiday, try to stick to your dog's diet as closely as possible. If it can't handle other foods, take a supply with you from home. However, the major brands of food are widely available, even in other countries.

Aggression while eating
It's not unusual for a dog to defend its food bowl while eating. It will do this by displaying aggressive (i.e. dominant!) behaviour. During the first few months, regularly remove the bowl while your dog is eating and replace it after thirty seconds. This action confirms your higher position in the hierarchy. If your pup growls or jumps at you, reprimand it. It's a good idea to do this occasionally when your dog is older too; your position in the pack must always be clear.

Snacks
Naturally, you will regularly want to spoil your dog with an extra treat. Don't give it pieces of cheese or sausage; these contain too

much salt and fat. Sweets and biscuits are bad for its teeth. Moreover, a dog quickly learns to beg and will pester you to death as soon as it even sees the biscuit tin! For those 'special' moments there are various products in the shops that a dog will enjoy, and which are also healthy, even for its teeth. You will find a wide assortment of varying quality in the pet shop.

The butcher's left-overs

The bones of slaughtered animals have traditionally been given to the dog, and dogs are crazy about them, but they are not without risks. Pork and poultry bones are too weak. They can splinter and cause serious injury to the intestines. Beef bones are more suitable, but they must first be cooked to kill off dangerous bacteria. Pet shops carry a range of smoked, cooked and dried abattoir residue, such as pigs' ears, bull penis, tripe sticks, oxtails, gullet, dried muscle meat, and hoof chews.

Buffalo or cowhide chews

Dog chews are mostly made of beef or buffalo hide. Chews are usually knotted or pressed hide. Chews are usually knotted or pressed hide and can come in the form of little shoes, twisted sticks, lollies, balls and various other shapes; nice to look at and a nice change.

Munchy sticks

Munchy sticks are green, yellow, red or brown coloured sticks of various thickness. They consist of ground buffalo hide with a number of undefined additives.

The composition and quality of these between-meal treats is not always clear. Some are fine, but there have also been sticks found to contain high levels of cardboard and even paint residues. Choose a product whose ingredients are clearly described.

Fresh meat

Should you want to give your puppy fresh meat occasionally, never give it raw, but always boiled or roasted. Raw (or not fully cooked) pork or chicken can contain life-threatening bacteria. Chicken can be contaminated by the notorious salmonella bacteria, while pork can carry the Aujeszky virus. This disease is incurable and will quickly lead to the death of your pet.

Drinking

A dog must always have fresh drinking water available, and it won't do it any harm to give it milk once in a while, but remember that this contains calcium. Be careful during the first year; too much milk can distort the calcium/kiljoules balance in its food. Give your puppy only skimmed or semi-skimmed milk. Most dogs can't handle the fat contained in full-cream milk; it gives them diarrhoea.

Never give your dog ice-cold water after a hefty romp; it can cause stomach torsion!

Caring for your puppy

Proper (daily) care is extremely important for your puppy. A well cared-for dog has much less chance of becoming ill. Caring for a dog is not only necessary, but is also fun. You and your dog are giving each other some attention and it's an excellent moment for a game and a cuddle.

Coat

At an age of eight to twelve weeks, a puppy is like a disarming little bear with woolly fur. The baby coat is quickly replaced by the final coat, starting at the tail and slowly creeping forward to the head, until the whole coat has been replaced. Get your puppy used to a grooming session from the start. This keeps skin and hair in good condition, and you'll have less bother with dog's hairs in the house. There's a big difference between long and shorthaired dogs. Longhaired dogs must be brushed regularly. Brushing shorthaired dogs too often can lead to skin irritations and extreme hair loss.

Use a hard brush to brush out loose hairs. A second brushing with a soft brush will ensure a glossy coat. During the moulting season (twice a year), a fairly fine comb or brush will do good service. With these you can easily brush the undercoat (which comes loose during moulting) out of the upper coat. Longhaired dogs may even need to be brushed twice a day during the moulting season. The loose hair itches, causing the dog to bite and scratch itself. This can cause coat or skin damage. Outside the moulting season, brushing frequency is strongly dependent on the breed and coat structure.

Tangles can develop on longhaired dogs, especially behind the ears, on the chest and in the breech (the long hairs on the back of the legs and rear quarters). If these tangles get too big, clip them away. Never try to pull them free with a comb; this will certainly teach your dog to hate its grooming sessions!

Eyes

A dog's eyes should be cleaned regularly. Discharge gets into the corners of the eye. You can easily remove them by wiping them downward with your thumb. If you don't like doing that, use a piece of tissue or toilet paper.

Keeping your dog's eyes clean will take only a few seconds a day, so do it every day. If the discharge becomes yellow this could point to an irritation or infection. Eye drops (from your vet) will quickly solve this problem.

Ears

The ears are often forgotten when caring for dogs, but they must be cleaned at least once a week. This should preferably be done with a clean cotton cloth, moistened with lukewarm water or baby oil. Cotton wool is not suitable due to the fluff it can leave behind. **NEVER** penetrate the ear canal with an object. If you neglect cleaning your dog's ears there's a substantial risk of infection. A dog that is constantly scratching at its ears might be suffering from dirty ears, an ear infection or ear mites. This makes a visit to the vet essential.

Teeth

At the beginning, puppies have lovely, sharp white teeth. Plaque

manifests itself later as a yellow-brown coating on the teeth (usually at the gum) and can cause bad breath on a dog. It must be removed by a vet. Clean your dog's teeth at least once every two months to prevent plaque as far as possible. Clean the teeth with a small brush and some lukewarm water. Get your puppy used to this at an early age, otherwise dental care will become an unpleasant experience for it (and for you). The puppy must let you work in its mouth. This can be very important in other situations later. Poor dental care can lead to bad breath and gum infections.

Feed your dog primarily hard food, bones and chews, such as Nylabone.

These will keep the formation of plaque to a minimum.

Check your dog's teeth regularly, even if it doesn't show any signs of problems. Have any damage to teeth or jaws seen to by the vet, to prevent loss of important parts of the teeth.

Nails

On a dog that regularly walks on hard surfaces, its nails usually grind themselves down. In this case there's usually no need to clip their nails, but it wouldn't do any harm to check their length regularly. Using a piece of paper, you can easily see whether its nails are too long. If you can push the paper between the nail and the ground when the dog is standing,

then the nail is the right length. Nails that are too long can bother a dog. It can injure itself when scratching, so they must be kept trimmed. You can buy special nail clippers in pet shops. Be careful not to clip back too far as you could damage the skin around the nail, which can bleed heavily. If you feel unsure, have this necessary task done by a vet or an animal beauty parlour.

With some breeds, special attention is needed for the nail on the side of the fore or rear paws, the so-called dewclaw. This doesn't touch the ground and thus never gets ground down. Clip this nail regularly, otherwise your dog may catch it on something.

In the bath

You usually won't have to wash a dog very often. A well-cared for puppy won't get dirty very quickly. But even the cleanest dog will sometimes roll in something that stinks. Then a good wash with dog shampoo is needed. Use a disinfectant shampoo where possible to kill any parasites. Rinse out the foam well with clean water. Only let your dog outside when it's properly dry; even dogs can catch a cold!

The phases of your puppy's life

A lot of scientific research has been done into the effects that experiences in a young dog's life can have on its behavioural development. From this we know that a dog's behaviour is influenced to a high degree by positive and negative impulses from its surroundings.

If certain experiences are missed, this in itself can lead to behavioural disorders. A balanced and consistent upbringing is of great importance, but you must first understand at what moment you can successfully influence a certain aspect of your puppy's behaviour to give it such an upbringing. Behavioural scientists distinguish between the following phases of a puppy's development into an adult dog.

Vegetative phase (0-2 weeks)
This first phase in life lasts until about the time the puppies' eyes open and is purely vegetative; the puppies don't yet react consciously. They drink and then discharge the products of their digestion (stool and urine). But they can't yet do this themselves; the mother

licks her babies' tummies almost constantly to keep this process going.

The puppies find her teats by an inborn instinct, which you can observe up to about the tenth day: the urge to search. They move their heads backwards and forwards, while crawling around in circles. They soon find a part of their mother's body and, a little later, her teats. While drinking, they paw at the area around the teat with their forepaws in rhythmic movements. This 'milking' forms the basis for offering their paw later. During this vegetative phase the pups lie close against each other or their mother to sleep. If they lose this contact and don't find it again at once, they start to complain loudly.

Transition phase (2-3 weeks)

The hearing and optical nerves now start to develop. The eyes open, on average, between the twelfth and fifteenth day, but the pups can't yet see and can only distinguish between light and dark. Their eyesight is fully developed by the 21st day. From the sixteenth to eighteenth day, the pups can smell properly and start to sniff at their brothers and sisters. Towards the end of the third week, they start to growl and sometimes even to bark. The mother will eject half-digested food for her young now and then, when they press at the corners of her mouth (although this primeval behaviour has now disappeared with most pedigree bitches).

Imprinting phase (3-7 weeks)

The pups can now run pretty well (even if a little tottery). In the wild, the young first leave the nest around the 21st day. A new phase in their life now begins. External influences were insignificant up to now, but now a period of learning begins. Scientific research has shown that puppies will develop into totally shy, wild dogs if they don't have contact with humans between the fourth and seventh week of their life. Any attempts to establish a close relationship with a puppy after the seventh week will come to nothing. The only thing to do is to "tame" the puppies (like wild animals) with plenty of patience.

They can indeed overcome their fear of humans, but will never establish a real friendship.

Contact means not only seeing people, but also sniffing at them, cuddling and, especially, playing with them. This must be with men, women and children. If a puppy only has contact with women, it will often later be afraid of men. Imprinting is not only important in terms of humans. A young dog must make acquaintances with other dogs, objects, sounds, different situations and other animal varieties. If a puppy has only had contact with humans, and not (or not enough) with other dogs, then it can quickly become focussed on humans and won't know how to behave with other dogs later. This can even lead to sexual disorders and aggressive behaviour. Dogs that live in the wild learn about everything that they will be confronted with in later life from about the third week on. This means that your puppy should now also be making the acquaintance of all kinds of things that it will be confronted with as an adult dog. It is striking in this period how puppies imitate older dogs. This knowledge can be helpful in explaining anxiety behaviour.

Socialisation phase (7-12 weeks)

Up till now, the puppy was allowed to do everything it wanted, but now things will change. Not only in the wild, but also with

domesticated dogs, the father (or mother) begins to act as the trainer in a very authoritative manner. The puppy looks to and recognises its father as the natural leader of the pack. A dog that doesn't recognise its master as authority will be an animal that is difficult to handle. This is its form of protest, but this is often not understood. Just at the time that a puppy is taking its place in human society, it must learn to respect the human as trainer and authority. This means that, even when playing with its master, he can and may never win against him. Make sure your puppy plays with other dogs from time to time, otherwise it becomes a human's dog. This will cause problems when out walking; it may be aggressive or anxious in the presence of other dogs. This is also just the right time to start house-training your puppy, and you can show it the things it must respect; table and chair-legs, carpets, toys laying around, shoes etc. Of course, there must be one or two things it is allowed to get at, such as a bone or some toys of its own.

Between its eighth and tenth week, a puppy experiences a period of emotional instability, where impressions of fear can easily be formed. It helps not to confront the pup with unknown impressions during this phase. The attaching of an identification chip, for example, should be done before your puppy reaches eight weeks. Delay any visit to the vet's for a while too, if this is possible.

Hierarchical phase (12-16 weeks)

In the wild, this phase is characterised primarily by confirmation of the hierarchy amongst the puppies themselves. This first happens with physical power, but later by recognition of self-assurance and personality. This is the best moment to begin with simple exercises, such as sitting on command, or retrieving a ball. These exercises confirm the hierarchy and your puppy will be more obedient. You can teach it to sit by softly pushing its hindquarters to the ground while calling the command "Sit!" preceded by its name. Then you reward it abundantly, after all it did sit down even if you did the work for it. By repeating this regularly, the puppy will understand the intention itself within a few days. You use similar methods to teach it other commands and get fastest results with lots of praise. Never punish a puppy for not doing what you want!

Pack order phase (16-24 weeks)

In this period, you can extend the obedience exercises and really start serious training. This doesn't mean you can now start yelling and snapping at it. You will achieve much more with friendly but firm treatment and lots of

rewards. Never make the mistake of trying to estimate your dog's intelligence by the time it needs to master an exercise. This says nothing about its intelligence. It's more likely to be a specific characteristic of its breed. A sheepdog bred for subjection and obedience will learn to lay down on command far faster than a Newfoundland terrier that has lived independently for centuries. At the age of about four or five months, a puppy will experience a second period of emotional instability. Even if it's been well socialised and has no fear of people, strong reactions can occur when it's faced with sudden changes to its familiar surroundings. Physical punishment is now even more out of the question than ever. A dog,

at this age, has no real way it can mentally process this, and the after-effects of such punishment will be intense. During this period too, try to avoid going to the vet's with your puppy.

Puberty phase (24 weeks up to sexual maturity)

The puberty phase doesn't produce much that's new. The experiences that the pup has had during the previous phases of its life are now expanded upon, and intensified. Stick to the obedience exercises, but don't overdo it. If this is your first dog, you should really attend an obedience course with it. There you can teach your puppy, with the help of an experienced dog-lover, to cross the 't's and dot the 'i's.

A place of its own

Your puppy has a right to its own part of your home. It's advisable to find a place that is not in everybody's way.

You can then send your puppy to its place when you need to. Sending it 'to its place' must become part of its training programme.

You can obtain the fastest results (if you need to do this) by taking it to its place while frequently repeating "basket" followed by "Stay!" After some time you can do the exercise by using the command "Basket!" and pointing to its place with your hand. In the end you will only need to use the command "Basket!"

A puppy must feel safe in its own place, so leave it in peace as soon as it starts to go there on its own (no children in the basket, and no more games). A dog prefers a cool place to sleep. It doesn't feel the

cold quickly, but will quickly be bothered by heat. Its sleeping place must be draught-free. Never put a wet dog in a cold place, only a dry coat offers enough insulation.

Kennel

Many dog owners have a kennel. This can be outside or inside the house. The question whether it's good to keep a dog in a kennel is not easy to answer. Some people keep their dogs in an outdoor kennel most of the day, others use an indoor kennel for it to sleep in at night. Between these two extremes, there's a whole scale of alternatives.
If a dog has to spend practically all day in an outdoor kennel, it becomes a prison. Dogs are pack animals and will not be happy in solitary confinement. But a ken-

nel (indoors or out) can also be a nice place for your dog to be, if used in moderation. It can be a safe place for it to eat, drink, sleep and even to spend the night.

A kennel can also be useful to you: If you do need to leave the dog alone at home, it's nice to know that it can't get up to any mischief.

Bringing you puppy up

Naturally, you're very happy with, and proud of, your new housemate. You surely let your cute and funny puppy happily do its own thing, don't you?

After all, there's still plenty of time for bringing it up! This attitude will lead to certain grief later. All the impressions a puppy gets during the imprinting and socialisation phases are stored in its memory. If it learns bad habits during these phases, you can practically never correct them at a later stage. You must teach your puppy the elementary things (such as obedience and house-training) as quickly as possible.

The first thing a puppy needs is clarity: what it may do and what not. If it may do something, it may always do it: if it must not do something, then it must never do it! You're not just sometimes the boss, but either always or never. A dog is used to living in a certain hierarchy, and it must always be clear that you and your family are higher in the pecking order than the puppy. You must be consistent, clear and persistent.

House-training

House-training will cost a lot of your time at first, but you can't avoid it. Every puppy has to be house-trained; it's the first phase of its upbringing. Keep a close eye on your puppy for the first two weeks. Every time it wakes up, eats, drinks or plays, take it to a fixed place outside the house where it can do its business. Pick a place where it can also take care of its needs later, such as between bushes. Reprimand it if it does its business on the pavement; that's a no-no. If it does, then clean up after it. You can buy special paper bags and shovels to do this job while keeping your hands clean. If your puppy appears restless, walks around in circles or otherwise shows the need relieve itself, take it outside immediately. Sometimes, this can be tedious; the puppy has to do its business, but is suddenly distracted by all kinds of interesting things going on around it, and can sometimes forget what it came outside for. Wait and then praise it abundantly when it finally succeeds.

Don't react to 'accidents' in the house too strongly in the beginning. These will certainly happen because your puppy still has to learn. Reprimand it lightly, take it outside and give it the chance to deposit the rest. Spray a little disinfectant on the spot where the accident happened. What you must certainly never do is rub your puppy's nose in its droppings. This is pure animal cruelty; the puppy will only be frightened and it won't learn a thing from it. Furthermore, you can permanently damage its sense of smell.

With the night in mind, don't give a puppy anything to drink after eight o'clock in the evening. It still can't hold its bladder very long. Walk it one more time before bedtime, so it can empty its bladder a last time. In the early days, take a puppy out at least every two hours (except at night!), and then gradually increase the time between walks. How quickly your puppy becomes house-trained depends entirely on you. Be alert, patient and reward it when things go well.

Fact!
Don't be concerned if your young male doesn't lift its leg when urinating. He will only do this when he's sexually mature (at an age of around nine months).

Destructiveness
Your puppy will doubtless feel the urge to chew on anything and everything at a certain moment. However annoying this may be, it's a logical effect of its teeth changing. This happens at around three to five months. The changing teeth cause itching and pain in the jaws. The puppy tries to relieve the pain and speed up the change process by gnawing on something. The command "Stop it!" is often enough to actually stop it (even if only briefly). Give your puppy a dog chew of buffalo hide, or a hard toy that it can work on.

With young dogs, destructive behaviour can be the result of boredom. A puppy must always be able to play, it's a key to its development. If it gets too little attention, it will search for something to do itself. It will start to chew on (and disappear with) the first thing that comes to its mind. With some insight into your puppy's experience of the world, you

can indeed keep this destructive-ness under control. Imagine the following: your puppy comes to you with an old slipper that it's just found. You find that clever and let it chew up the slipper, after all it's only an old one. A few days later, you find it's been at your expensive new shoes. This time you're furious, but in your puppy's logic, there's no differen-ce at all between the old slipper and your expensive new shoes. It also won't know the difference between a machine-made table-cloth and a hand-woven Persian carpet. Your puppy doesn't under-stand terms like cheap or expensi-ve, so make sure it may only play with things meant for it (a ball, a chew or a toy). If you do want to let your puppy chew on an old shoe or cloth, then make every effort to make sure it understands precisely what 'its' shoe or cloth is. However there'll always be a risk it will forget!

If you want to make absolutely sure your puppy doesn't destroy the sofa, then use an indoor ken-nel. If it has to sleep and eat there, it will soon regard it as its own place and will go in without protest.

Walking on the lead
The first time your puppy is put on the lead, it will certainly find it unusual and protest. This is ano-ther new experience for it to get used to. Walking on the lead is sometimes also called 'walking at

heel'. Practise this with your puppy on the lead at first (later, it can also follow you at heel wit-hout the lead). Have it walk on your left so that your right hand is free. Only start practising after your puppy has done its business and has played a little. Then it won't be a barrel of unspent ener-gy. Find a quiet place where it won't be too easily distracted. If your puppy dawdles, stands still or runs too fast, correct it with a tug on the lead and the command 'heel!' Again, don't forget to prai-se it and cuddle it once in a while when everything goes well. Don't expect wonders from this exercise, you're still dealing with a puppy after all. Take your time and don't make the practice sessions too long. Practising playfully and enthusiastically a couple of times each time you go out (with abun-dant rewards!) will bring the best results in the end.

Dogs usually run happily to the door as soon as their master picks up their lead, but sometimes your puppy might not feel like going out. If it refuses to walk with you, give it a gentle tug on the lead. Never drag it behind you, because then it will only find walking on the lead an unpleasant event.

Once a puppy has mastered wal-king on the lead, and understands there's no point in refusing to go, then it will try another trick. It will start to pull at the lead. You

can correct this too with short tugs on the lead and the command 'heel!' or 'walk!'. Whatever commands you choose is completely up to you, but keep them short and never change them again. Make sure different commands don't sound alike; a dog responds to a sound, and not to what you say.

Once walking goes well in quiet streets, then look for a busier area. Keep the exercises short for the time being. Five intensive minutes with your puppy are enough.
Stay calm, and speak praisingly to it. Your voice is a great support in any situation.
Now it's time to cross the 't's and dot the 'i's. Shorten the lead until your dog's head is parallel with your knees. If it stays back, give it a little tug on the lead with the command 'heel!' or 'walk!'. If it tries to walk too far ahead (which is more often the case), do the same thing. When this is going well, you loosen the lead out again, but keep correcting as soon as your pup makes a mistake.

Coming on command

To teach a dog to come on command, you again pick a short command, such as 'come!' or 'here!' Start practising this with your puppy on a long (roll-up) lead. Call its name. If you see it's looking at you and giving you its attention, call the command. If it doesn't come immediately, give it

a little tug on the lead and entice it to come. Here too, friendliness and reward will get the best results. Impatient shouting and punishment will eventually lead to a shy dog.

Every time your pup strays away from a straight line on its way to you, correct it by gently pulling on the lead. Praise and cuddle it abundantly when it gets to you. Once in a while give it a dog biscuit for its performance.
As long as you have your puppy on the lead, this exercise will deliver fast results. But it will become more difficult when it's running free. Give it the time to learn!
In the same way, you can practice standing at the pavement edge, which is important for road safety. You must make your dog stop and sit at the edge of any pavement. If you have to cross a lot of roads during your daily walk, this is perhaps a tedious way to walk, but a safe one. A dog that suddenly runs into the road is a danger to itself and others.

Again: every exercise will demand patience. Sometimes, it can take months before you're sure your dog won't suddenly run onto the road, and actually does come when you call it. Calm and reward remain the fastest route to success. Never forget that these exercises are a serious business for you, but no more than a game for your puppy, so don't practice too fanatically and always keep it playful. A puppy will learn best when it's having fun!

Chasing cats

It's also funny watching a woolly young puppy in full chase behind a cat, but you must try to suppress these instincts from the beginning. A young dog must learn to control its hunting instincts. If it's now allowed to chase the chickens or the neighbour's cat, it will later chase anything that tries to escape from it. Ideally, you should get a kitten at the same time as your puppy and let them grow up together. Your dog will then be used to cats and won't regard them as a natural enemy. It's a common misnomer that dogs and cats can't get along with each other.

Never make the mistake of provoking or waking your puppy's assumed aggression towards cats. You are creating a problem that in fact does not exist. If your dog does react by standing tensely when it sees a cat, be firm. Reprimand it and use your strictest command. This is an excellent example of a moment when you must demonstrate your authority!

Always try to react totally neutral to all other animals, but especially towards cats (after all, these are the animals your dog will come up against most often in a town). Never allow your dog to chase any animal, whatever it is.

Punishment and reward

Rewarding is the most important aspect of bringing up a puppy. It gets a positive buzz whenever it's obeyed a command. A reward certainly doesn't need to always be something tasty. A cuddle, a word of praise or a game will motivate your puppy just as well.

But despite an up-bringing based on the reward principle, your puppy will sometimes get up to things where a friendly approach just won't work. Then it must be punished, but hitting it, locking it up in a shed or tying it to something are poor ways to punish a puppy. In fact, if you do use such methods, you can expect a shy and nervous dog.

A good grumble or ticking off is usually enough. If you then ignore your puppy for a while, it will regard this as a strict punishment. If this doesn't do the trick, then you have go to back into your puppy's heritage. In the wild, the mother dog picks up a puppy by the scruff of its neck with her teeth, and lifts it off the ground. The pup will regard this experience as a punishment for something it's done wrong.

By punishing a puppy this way, you're imitating the behaviour of its mother. Grab the puppy's coat at the neck, pick it up from the ground and tick it off. But don't make the mistake of picking it up and shaking it. Grabbing at the neck and shaking is part of its

hunting instinct, a method of killing the prey. Your puppy will get totally mixed up if you use this unnatural method of correction.

When you let your dog go again, its whimpering and submissive posture will show that it's understood its punishment. It goes down, and sits quietly watching you with its tail between its legs. Don't go soft and start consoling your puppy straight away, as that negates the punishment, but staying angry for a long period doesn't help either. The best thing is to let it see you're dissatisfied with it for a few more minutes.

Punishment only makes sense if you do it at the moment your puppy misbehaves. Imagine you come home and find that your puppy has been chewing at the sofa. You get angry and punish your pup. This happens two or three times. The fourth time you come home, your puppy won't greet you, but will creep away in fear. You've created a link between your coming home and punishment. It will keep chewing at the sofa, because your puppy doesn't connect the punishment with that at all. In its mind, it gets punished when it greets you at the door.

Another example: you're in the park and want to show off to some friends how clever your puppy is. Normally it always obeys you, but now you find it won't come to you when called. You feel embarrassed and shout louder and louder. After a while, your puppy comes to you, unaware of having done anything wrong. You want to show your friends that you're not going to let a puppy make a mockery of you by giving it a good telling-off. This is the worst thing you can do. The dog sees this punishment as its reward for coming to you. The next time you call it, it may not come at all, because the last reward it got for coming to you is still fresh in its memory. In cases where your puppy only obeys after repeated calls, you must still praise it for its good work. Just keep hoping that it will get better with time.

Timid behaviour

In some situations your puppy will behave timidly. This is sometimes useful because it may prevent accidents (fear of fire or traffic). In other cases this fearful behaviour can produce its own problems. If your dog is frightened of storms, it won't go out and may do its business in the house. If it's afraid of an open umbrella, you'll get soaked to the skin every time you go out with it in the rain. If you notice this kind of anxious behaviour, you must reprimand it. If that doesn't work you must punish it. This may sound strange, but if you console and cuddle it, you'll only achieve the opposite to what you really want. In its experience, your consolation is a reward for its anxious behaviour, and this will just get worse. So reprimand your dog when it's frightened for no reason. Try to convince it that there's nothing wrong, for example by letting it sniff at the umbrella to convince itself that this is not about to attack it.

One of the best known forms of fear in a dog is that of fireworks. Many pets go into total panic, but a puppy that's been properly socialised, and has learned to deal with loud bangs in its early youth, won't be afraid of fireworks. Police and hunting dogs are specially trained to be 'gunsure'. Many dog training schools use bangers or starting pistols during their courses. If your young dog does get frightened by a bang, don't console it. Ignore its fear. Consoling it will only confirm its suspicion that a loud bang is something to be afraid of. Dogs base their behaviour on that of their master; if you totally ignore the bang, your dog will do the same in the end.

Car journeys

Most dogs enjoy car journeys, not because of the car itself, but because it means that the whole family is going somewhere nice. Some dogs, however, never get used to the car and are sick every time. This can be annoying if you need to take it to the vet's or to a dog show. There's nothing you can do except to lay out a plastic sheet on the back seat and to drive as carefully as possible.

Get your puppy used to the car from an early age by taking it out for short trips twice a week. Then let it out somewhere nice and play with it. Thus it will learn to connect car journeys with something to look forward to, and will then enjoy them. Then drive quietly home. Gradually lengthen the journeys, so that after a few weeks you're going on quite long trips together.

Always take a towel, kitchen roll and a plastic bag with you as a precaution. You will notice when your pup is car-sick and needs to vomit. First the skin around its nose will become damp. Then it will open its mouth and breathe quickly with its tongue hanging out. At this stage you can still do something about it. Stop the car and go for a short walk with your puppy. If you can't stop, you will notice that the moistness around its mouth gets worse. It will begin to dribble in long streams. The

puppy is obviously feeling uncomfortable and will soon be sick.

Punishment certainly won't help here; it only confirms that travelling in a car is something unpleasant, and you can expect the same thing next time. Always show your puppy that a ride in the car is something to enjoy by your own behaviour. Never drag it into the car on its lead; let it sit on someone's lap (especially the first few trips) and speak with it calmly as you drive. If your puppy stays car-sick despite all your efforts, it will probably remain so. Unfortunately, tablets against carsickness don't always work. Don't feed an adult dog for about six hours before you leave. Go for a long walk just before you depart,

and adjust your driving to the situation (no sudden braking, sharp bends or strong acceleration). A dog that suffers from car-sickness will prefer it if you drive at a constant speed in highest gear.

Leaving your dog alone

No dog likes being left alone, but sometimes there's no choice. Your puppy needs to get used to it too. First leave it alone by simply going out of the room. Reward it abundantly if things go well. The next step may be going out into the garden, and then you can slowly extend your absences. At first stay close by, and if it starts barking or howling, you can quickly respond with a reprimand, "Quiet!". Then leave it alone again. If it starts again, repeat the ritual. It's important to build this exercise up slowly. If the dog stays quiet for ten minutes while you're still somewhere in the house, then you can start going outside. If you're on good terms with your neighbours, ask them if they heard anything and if so, at what time. In this case, your puppy was not yet ready for you to be away quite that long. Next time try to make your absence a little shorter.

New experiences

Once your puppy has got used to things around it and walks confidently around outside, start taking it to places that are a little more busy (public parks, shopping streets or the railway station). Give it time to look around at what's happening, and let strangers stop it once in a while. Most people love puppies, and yours will always be welcomed too, but on the other hand all this attention should not distract it from its new experiences. The right balance is important.

Your puppy must get used to such things as loud and strange noises (fast traffic, sirens, horns). It must not be frightened of them. If it does act frightened, calm it with your voice and body talk. If things

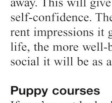

go well, tie your puppy to a post, and go and stand a little further away. This will give your puppy self-confidence. The more different impressions it gets in its early life, the more well-balanced and social it will be as an adult dog.

Puppy courses

If you've not had a lot of experience in bringing up a dog, then a puppy course is to be recommended. You and your puppy can playfully learn to get on together. You will also learn that things you believe you are doing well can be done better with no extra effort. Don't be disappointed if you don't get results at once. Stay patient and stay friendly. After a while, you will see that your puppy has learned the necessary after all. In principle, a puppy can take part in a puppy course once it's had all its injections (around twelve weeks). Don't let puppies of larger breeds romp too much, or too wildly, with other puppies because of the risk of hip or elbow dysplasia.

Puppies and older dogs

If you bring a puppy into your home when you already have another dog (or dogs), you must reckon with changes within the pack. Give your other dog the time to get used to the puppy. Dogs can quickly become jealous, so make sure the older dog still gets as much love and attention as before. Never give it the feeling that it's suddenly the second priority.

If you divide your love and attention honestly, things will be fine. If both dogs eat in the same room, stay with them until they're finished eating. Make sure each dog eats only from it's own bowl and that they don't steal from each other.

You can avoid problems by being consistent with both dogs. Remember that the puppy will view the older dog as an example. Young animals learn by imitating

their elders. If the older dog has negative character traits (shyness, begging or aggressiveness), the puppy may copy them. Try to prevent contact with these characteristics as far as possible. If the older dog is a normally developed and well-behaved animal, the contact between it and the puppy will have a positive influence on the young one's upbringing

Never practice training exercises with both dogs together; you will not succeed. Your older dog has 'grandfather' rights. Go out with it first and then bring it home, and go out with the puppy for a quarter of an hour. You can practice together with your partner and both dogs, but practice has shown, especially during more difficult exercises, that one of the dogs will feel compelled to look for the other. This is bad for its concentration. However walking both dogs out together with your partner can work well.

Play and exercise

If you, as master, want to make a good impression on your dog, you must play with it a lot.

If your dog likes you, then there will be a strong bond and good contact between you. But a game is also an opportunity for the dog to test its strengths against yours. So you must always be the one to say when playing starts and when it finishes. This way you confirm your position at the top of the pecking order. Only use a toy that you bring out to play with together. The dog must never be able to play with this on its own! A knotted piece of thick rope is a good idea.

Dogs need to play with each other when they're young. We observe these games mostly with animals with a relatively long parenting period (such as wolves). With pets, the long-term parenting by the mother can not be replaced by playing with the other animals in the pack, because they're simply not there. Humans must take over this task. Dogs get all kinds of experiences through play in their early youth, in fact playing represents their first lessons in life. In play, their skills improve and they become stronger. Puppies beam with obvious joy when they're playing. They are, after all, social animals that make their first contacts with their counterparts in play. These contacts are indispensable for a happy and healthy dog's life.

Forms of play
We can clearly distinguish between a number of different forms of a puppy's play. These are something like 'preparatory exercises' for adulthood.

The hunt

In this form of play one puppy cowers behind another as if preparing to attack. However the 'hunter' does not attack its 'victim' as if it were prey or an enemy. The roles are also often switched and the hunted starts to pursue the hunter. This hunting game is clearly something different from when cats cower behind each other. That is not play with a companion, but indeed the hunting of a prey.

The fight

During a fight game, puppies often seem quite aggressive: they show their teeth. A lot of biting goes on but not serious biting. Assertiveness comes to the fore in fighting games; positions in the hierarchy are being set. The weaker animal submits by lying on its back (a sign of subjection). Snouts are often bitten during this game. A puppy grasps its opponent's snout in its mouth, but doesn't bite hard. The fighting game is preparation for the seriousness of later life and is part of your dog's character formation.

Pseudo-sexual play

During this form of play, puppies appear to try to mate with each other. However this is only imitation that has nothing to do with any real urge to reproduce. Males will also try to cover another male.

Sensory play

With this form of play, puppies practice the use of their senses. They splash in puddles, dive into mud pools and roll in dirt and cow-pats. Even if you're not that delighted when your dog comes home stinking and filthy, let it go its own way as far as you can. These games (however filthy) teach a puppy about the world around it.

Exercise

A dog needs plenty of exercise. How much exactly depends on the breed, of course. You won't have to walk as far with a small poodle as with an Alsatian. But don't overdo things with a young puppy, especially those of breeds that are vulnerable to HD and ED. Begin with very short walks and gradually increase the distance. The way the puppy behaves must always be the barometer in terms of the length of a walk. If it starts to show motions to lie down, it wants to rest, and you should respect that. Whatever you do, don't try to drag it along behind you. Several short walks a day are better for muscle building than one long one. A good guideline is six to eight times a day for five to ten minutes.

Of course, a dog can walk longer when it's somewhat older. Once it's adult it can walk just as much and just as far as it (and you!) can manage. Don't worry if your

puppy lies flat on the grass with its tongue hanging out after a game. Just like a human, a dog keeps its body temperature at the right level by evaporation of moisture, but a dog perspires only through small glands on the soles of its feet. All the other moisture evaporates through its mouth.

Ensure that your puppy learns to walk properly. During the first year keep it mostly on the lead, so that it's more or less forced to walk in a straight line. Straight-line movements are good for building muscle in the hindquarters. Try to prevent your dog walking at an amble, i.e. its paws on the right or left side of its body move backwards and forwards together. Seen from behind the dog appears to be waddling; it has a slovenly gait (in dog shows, the amble gait

is not permitted for most breeds). At a higher speed, a dog is walking correctly when the paws diagonally opposite each other move forward or backward together (for instance rear left together with fore right). Even if your puppy grows up on a farm and can run around freely most of the time, you still need to take it out on the lead a couple of times a day. It can then learn a good gait, and it will help its muscles develop optimally.

If you plan to go out on a bicycle with your dog beside you, let it get used to trotting beside the bike from a young age. Don't wait until your dog is nine months old, but start early and gradually build the distance up. Make sure the dog doesn't run beside the bike, but that it keeps to a trot. Remember that this should be a pleasure for both sides, overdoing things can do harm here too.

Walking up steps
Every dog has to learn to walk up and down stairs. It can be annoying when it stops at some steps and won't go any further. You can easily carry a puppy upstairs, but it's somewhat more difficult with a full-grown Great Dane! But walking up and down stairs also puts a very heavy burden on the joints in the hip and elbow regions, so keep it to an absolute minimum in the first year, especially for breeds that are vulnerable to HD and ED.

A dog and children

Children and dogs are the subject of many a sweet snapshot, but also of some gruesome stories. Many of these stories need never have been told. A dog won't bite a child just like that, but it will bite to defend itself if it feels threatened.

In most cases the dog ends up taking the blame, but often this is actually the fault of the adults, the dog's keepers and the parents of the child. They must teach their child how to behave with a dog, and it's also their job to bring up their dog consistently and to protect it against children that are still too young to understand the nature of a dog.

Toddlers and puppies

If you're thinking of taking in a dog while you also have a baby (or are expecting one), think about what you are about to do! Just like a baby, a puppy needs lots of attention in the first few months. Think about house-training, socialisation and up-bringing. After looking after a baby, will you still have the energy left to give a puppy all the attention it needs? Think about the drawbacks too, both of a baby and of a puppy. Imagine you have a baby that cries a lot, costing you precious sleep. How will you react when the puppy then does its business on the carpet, just when you were pleased to be able to sit down for a few minutes? A puppy may also be sickly at the beginning and will need extra attention. Do you still have the time and energy to be able to care for it?

Whether it's a good idea to get a dog at this time strongly depends on the situation. Someone who is experienced with dogs will view it differently to someone who is getting a dog for the first time. There are also advantages in getting a puppy while there's a baby in the house. By the time the baby is a toddler and starts to crawl, the dog is already practically grown up. Dog and child grow up together and are completely used to each other. Relating to the dog can also be a valuable contribution to a child's development.

Even when dog and child grow up together, there can still be potentially dangerous situations. A toddler may crawl up behind the dog. The toddler looks on with wide eyes as the dog keeps walking away, but the dog hates it. It goes to its basket in the corner of the room, and starts to warn the child by growling. The baby now finds the dog's noises even more interesting and tries to touch it, at which moment the dog bites.

Within the family, the dog is at the bottom of the pecking order. A young child is certainly not in a position to put a dog in its place. Only in the presence of the parents will a dog recognise the higher position in the hierarchy that the children around it occupy. Apart from that, small children are unpredictable and they still don't always understand the consequences of their actions. A toddler wants to investigate its surroundings. If it pulls a dog's ears or sticks it fingers in its eyes, the dog will make a noise. The toddler doesn't understand that it's hurting the dog, it's much more interested in pulling even harder.

Even the most trusted dog will eventually turn on the young explorer if this goes on too long. Try to avoid this kind of situation by never leaving young children alone with a dog! If you stick rigorously to this rule, then you can't even go upstairs any more when the child is crawling around in the living room and your dog is asleep in its basket. Avoid possible conflict situations. Don't let a child and dog hover around you together while you're busy preparing the dog's meal.

Training children

Just as a puppy must be trained when it joins the family, the children also need to learn a thing or two. You must never assume that they know how to handle a dog responsibly just like that. Teach them the following:
• To respect the dog from the beginning. A puppy is a living thing, and not a toy you can do

Misplaced pride

Children are always proud of their newest acquisition. Before you know it, all their friends have been invited to come round and admire their puppy on the first day. However understandable their enthusiasm is, you must temper it. Prepare the child properly for the arrival of its new housemate, and make it clear that the new member of the family is flesh and blood, and not a cuddly toy. It's vital for the puppy to get the chance to get to know its own family first, so wait a few days with all those visitors.

Children can be wild and agile, and a puppy can easily get frightened. Teach children to behave as calmly as possible with a puppy. Even if patience is not always a strongly developed feature of a child's nature, they must use it with their puppy. They have to learn that the puppy needs to learn too. Hitting and shouting are out of the question (not only for the children!).

Somewhat older children can help to feed and care for a dog. This must be accompanied by an adult, as a child is not in a position to take care of bringing up a dog alone. You can add tasks as the child gets older. Of course, children will want to flaunt their new dog, but a word of warning is due here: a child must be mentally and physically stronger

what you want with;
• handle the dog calmly;
• learn to understand the dog's language; what is it saying when in growls or wags its tail? A child must also learn to recognise when a dog is frightened;
• never to hit or pester a dog; if a dog feels pain, it will bite;
• how to cuddle the dog;
• to leave the dog in peace when it's asleep or in its basket;
• not to call commands or to call the dog's name when it's not appropriate;
• to let the dog come to it, rather than walking towards the dog;
• never to run up behind a dog;
• never to run towards a strange dog to cuddle it or give it something to eat. A dog may perceive a child running towards it as a threat, so approach it calmly. Always ask the owner first if your child can cuddle the dog or give it a treat.

than a dog before it can take it out without an adult!

Afraid of dogs?

Adults that are afraid of dogs often transfer their fear to their children. They will then hide screeching behind their mother or father, and then be consoled for the fact that they're afraid of that awful beast.

It is better, though, for parents to suppress their own fear and teach their children how to approach a (strange) dog. This also helps safeguard the child. A child running away from a dog shrieking in fear can make a dog aggressive or awake its hunting instincts, but if a child behaves normally and calmly (hands always held low!) nothing will normally happen.

Parasites

All dogs are vulnerable to various sorts of parasite. Parasites are tiny creatures that live at the expense of another animal. They feed on blood, skin or other body substances.

There are two main types. Internal parasites live within their host animal's body (tapeworm and roundworm) and external parasites live on the animals exterior, usually in its coat (fleas and ticks), but also in its ears (ear mites).

Fleas

Fleas feed on a dog's blood. They cause not only itching and skin problems, but can also carry diseases. In large numbers they can cause anaemia and dogs can also become allergic to a flea's saliva, which can cause serious skin conditions. So it's important to treat the dog for fleas as effectively as possible, not just on the dog itself but also its surroundings. For treatment on the animal, there are various medicines: drops for the neck and to put it in its food, flea collars, long-life sprays and flea powders. There are various sprays in pet shops that can be used to eradicate fleas in the dog's immediate surroundings. Choose a spray that kills both adult fleas and their larvae. If your dog goes in your car, you should spray that too. Fleas can also affect other pets, so you should treat those too.

Your vet and pet shop have a wide range of flea treatments and can advise you on the subject.

Ticks

Ticks are small, spider-like parasites. They feed on the blood of the animal or person they've settled on. A tick looks like a tiny, grey coloured leather bag with eight feet. When it has sucked itself full, it can easily be five to ten

Flea

times its own size and is darker in colour. Dogs usually fall victim to ticks in bushes, woods or long grass. Ticks cause not only irritation by their blood sucking but can also carry a number of serious diseases. This applies especially to the Mediterranean countries, which can be infested with blood parasites. In our country these diseases are fortunately less common. But Lymes disease, which can also affect humans, has reached our shores. Your vet can prescribe a special treatment if you're planning to take your dog to southern Europe. It is important to fight ticks as effectively as possible. Check your dog regularly, especially when its been running free in woods and bushes. It can also wear an anti-tick collar. Removing a tick is simple using a tick pincette. Grip the tick with the pincette, as close to the dog's skin as possible and carefully pull it out. You can also grip the tick between your fingers and, using a turning movement, pull it carefully out. You must disinfect the spot where the tick had been using iodine to prevent infection. Never 'suffocate' the tick in alcohol, ether or oil. In a shock reaction the tick may discharge the infected contents of its stomach into the dog's skin.

Worms

Dogs can suffer from various types of worm, The most common are tapeworm and roundworm.

Tapeworm causes diarrhoea and poor condition. With a tapeworm infection you can sometimes find small pieces of the worm around the dog's anus or on its bed. In this case, the dog must be wormed. You should also check your dog for fleas, which carry the tapeworm infection.

Roundworm is a condition that reoccurs regularly. Puppies are infected by their mother's milk. Roundworm causes problems such as diarrhoea, loss of weight and stagnated growth. In serious cases the pup becomes thin, but with a swollen belly. It may vomit and you can then see the worms in its vomit. They are spaghetti-like tendrils. A puppy must also be treated for worms regularly.

Tick

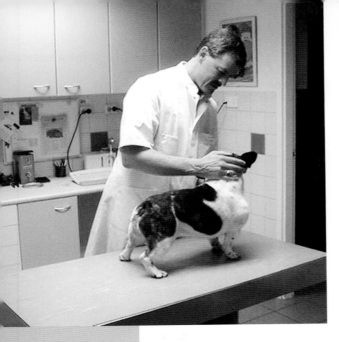

Vaccinations

Fleas, worms and ticks are pretty nasty little beasts, but at least they can be seen with the naked eye, and dogs can become much more seriously ill from invisible 'beasts'.

Therefore having your pet vaccinated is one of the most important elements of keeping it healthy. Dogs can be protected against a number of serious conditions by vaccination. Because the importance of vaccination can not be overstated, we'll cover a few diseases and their consequences here:

A puppy gets its first vaccination against distemper and parvovirus at six weeks. Six weeks later follows a second injection against these diseases and against infectious liver disease, Weil's disease and kennel cough. Four weeks later, it must be vaccinated against a number of these diseases again. At an age of three months, it can get its first injection against rabies. After these first vaccinations, injections are repeated annually in the form of a so-called 'cocktail injection".

Even dogs that never go out on the streets, but are allowed into the garden, must be vaccinated regularly. They can also come into contact with diseases in the garden. A lot of vets will send a reminder for the annual vaccination. The dates of these injections are registered in a special vaccination book and this will also serve as a reminder when the next vaccinations are due.

Vaccination plan
If you buy a puppy, the following vaccinations are mandatory:
At six weeks: Puppy vaccination
At nine weeks: Small cocktail (Parvo and Weil's disease)
At twelve weeks: Large cocktail

(Parvo, Distemper, Liver disease, Leptospirosis, Parainfluenza, Bordetella and possibly Rabies)

An adult dog (older than a year) must also be regularly vaccinated:
- In its second year: Small cocktail (and perhaps Rabies)
- In its third year: Large cocktail (and perhaps Rabies)
- In its fourth year: Small cocktail (and perhaps Rabies) and so on.

If your dog goes to a kennels while you're on holiday, it must be vaccinated against kennel cough. If you plan to take your dog abroad it must be vaccinated against rabies and registered with an electronic 'chip', otherwise it will have to go into six month's quarantine when you return to the UK. Your vet can advise you on the procedures, which need to be started well before your trip. Distemper is a highly infectious condition of the bronchial tracts and the intestines. It's a condition which gets rapidly worse and is usually fatal. Infectious liver disease is a virus that attacks the liver and is often fatal. Weil's disease is a serious condition that often ends fatally. Humans can also be infected. The chief symptoms are fever, jaundice and kidney infection. This disease is carried by the urine of infected rats in standing water, and by the urine of dogs which have become infected. Kennel cough in most cases is not dangerous, but is an unpleasant condition in the bronchial tracts, together with a hard, rough cough and retching. Parvo is a strong virus infection with often fatal consequences. The symptoms are heavy vomiting and diarrhoea with blood. Rabies is a virus which infects the nervous system and brain. If not treated quickly, this condition can also be fatal for humans. Rabies is transferred by the bite of an infected (wild) animal.

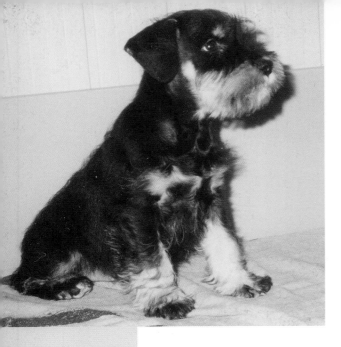

Usefull Addresses

People and Dogs Society (PADS)
Bernfold
45B Ashgap Lane
Normanton
West Yorkshire,
WF6 2DT, ENGLAND
Tel: +44 (0)1924-897732
    or +44 (0)1977-678593
Email: problems@padsonline.org
http://www.padsonline.org/

The Kennel Club
1 Clarges Street
London UK
W1J 8AB
Tel: 0870 606 6750
Fax: 020 7518 1058
http://www.the-kennelclub.org.uk/

The secretary General Scottish Kennel Club
Eskmills Park
Station Road
Musselborough EH21 7PQ
Tel: 0131 665 3920
Fax: 0131 653 6937
Email: info@scottishkennelclub.org
www.scottishkennelclub.org

The Irish Kennel Club Ltd.
Fottrell house,
Harold's
Cross Bridge,
Dublin 6W
Ireland
Tel: (01) 4533300 - 4532309 -
    4532310.
Fax: (01) 4533237
Email: ikenclub@indigo.ie
http://www.ikc.ie/

Other books from About Pets

- The Boxer
- The Border Collie
- The Cavalier King Charles Spaniel
- The Cocker Spaniel
- The Dalmatian
- The Dobermann
- The German Shepherd
- The Golden Retriever
- The Jack Russell Terrier
- The Labrador Retriever
- The Rottweiler
- The Budgerigar
- The Canary
- The Cockatiel
- The Parrot
- The Lovebird
- The Cat
- The Kitten
- The Dwarf Hamster
- The Dwarf Rabbit
- The Ferret
- The Gerbil
- The Guinea Pig
- The Hamster
- The Mouse
- The Rabbit
- The Rat
- The Goldfish
- The Tropical Fish
- The Snake

Key features of the series are:
- Most affordable books
- Packed with hands-on information
- Well written by experts
- Easy to understand language
- Full colour original photography
- 70 to 110 photos
- All one needs to know to care well for their pet
- Trusted authors, veterinary consultants, breed and species expert authorities
- Appropriate for first time pet owners
- Interesting detailed information for pet professionals
- Title range includes books for advanced pet owners and breeders
- Includes useful addresses, veterinary data, breed standards.

Tips

- Larger breeds of dogs are vulnerable to hip dysplasia. During its first year, you can do a lot to prevent the development of HD.

- An alarm clock can help your puppy through its first difficult nights.

- Never let your puppy run endlessly after a ball or stick.

- Don't let your puppy go up and down stairs for the first six months!

- Bring your dog up consistently. A puppy course is not just useful, but it's fun too.

- Give your puppy time to explore its new surroundings.

- Its first car journey is a real experience for a puppy. Make it a pleasant one.

- Never pick up a puppy by its forepaws.

- Don't just fight fleas, but their larvae too.

- Make sure your dog doesn't get too fat. Not too much food and plenty of exercise are the golden rules.

- Start early with brushing and combing so that your puppy gets used to it.

- Never let a puppy chase cats.

- Teach your puppy to eat different types of food, but make sure you feed it uniformly in the first few months.

- A puppy still has to learn everything. Be patient and don't rush things.

- If you can, pick up your puppy from the breeder in the morning.

- A puppy is not a toy!